Simon the Snake
A Christmas Story

Written and Illustrated
by Lori Kaiser

Another great book in the Xavier Series!

Published by
Carpe Diem Publishers
17401 Betty Blvd.
Canyon, TX 79015
806-433-6321

www.Carpediempublishers.com

© Copyright, 2011 by Carpe Diem Publishers. All Rights Reserved. No portion of this book may be reproduced, stored in a retrieval system, or transmitted, in any form or by any means, electronic, mechanical, photocopying, recording, or otherwise without prior written permission from publisher.
Printed in the United States of America
ISBN 978-0-9836651-3-7

To Uncle David,
who loved Christmas.
We miss you sooooo much!

But Simon loved Santa
and knew that one day,
He would help Santa,
a good Christmas make.

But all the elves were exhausted by Christmas Eve night.

Christmas Eve came,
and Santa loaded his sleigh.

"I'll get down those chimneys, somehow or some way."

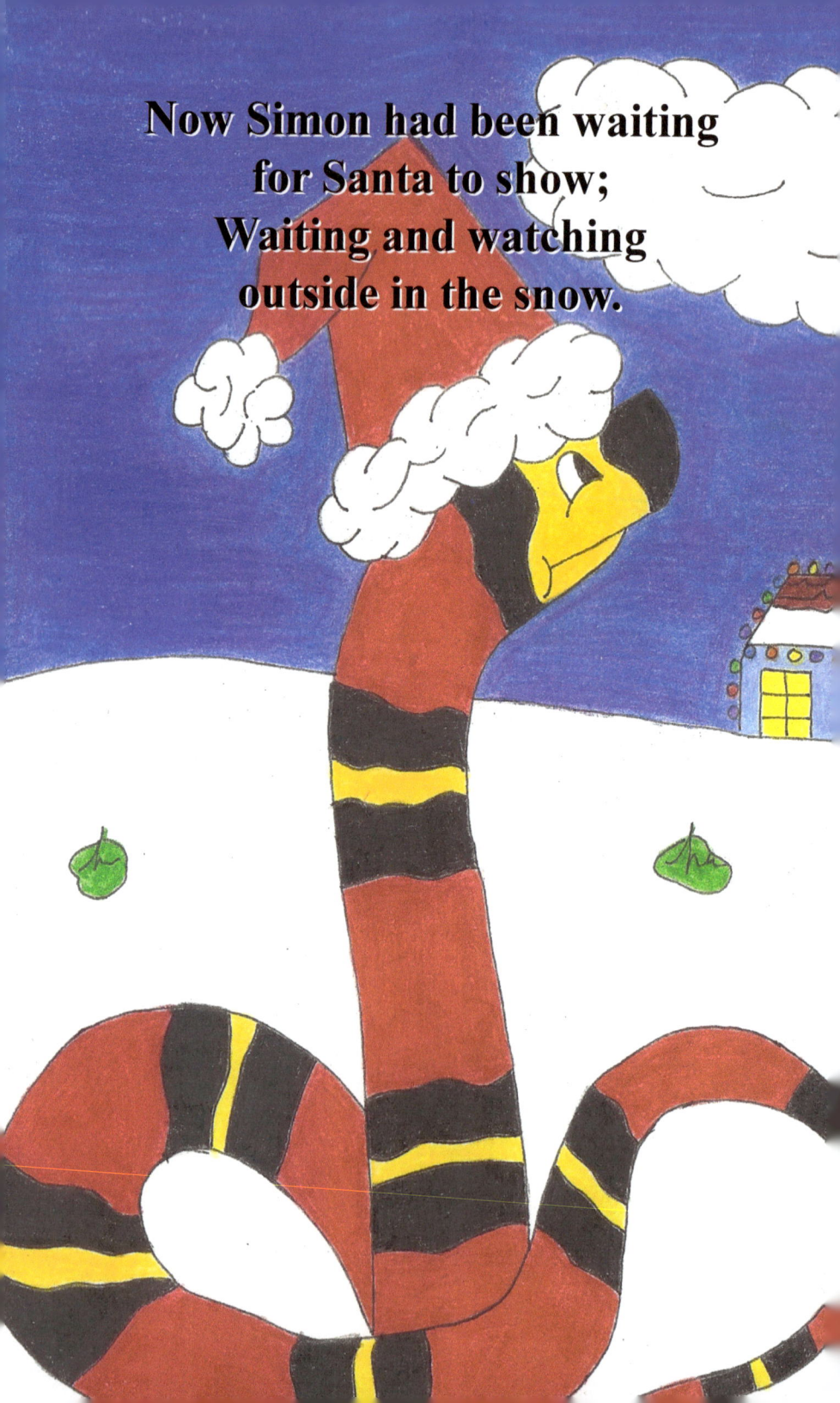

**Simon saw Santa
on a rooftop land.
When he got to the chimney,
he needed a hand.**

www.ingramcontent.com/pod-product-compliance
Lightning Source LLC
Chambersburg PA
CBHW042045290426
44109CB00001B/42